Build a Rain Barrel

BY SALLY MCGRAW · ILLUSTRATED BY ROGER STEWART

The Child's World®
childsworld.com

Published by The Child's World®
1980 Lookout Drive · Mankato, MN 56003-1705
800-599-READ · www.childsworld.com

Acknowledgments
The Child's World®: Mary Swensen, Publishing Director
Red Line Editorial: Editorial direction and production
The Design Lab: Design

Photographs ©: Shutterstock Images, 4, 7 (bottom), 8; Patrick
Foto/Shutterstock Images, 5; Yuri Samsonov/Shutterstock
Images, 7 (top); W. G. Design/Shutterstock Images, 9

Design Elements: JosephTodaro/Texturevault; Shutterstock Images

ISBN 9781503807877

LCCN 2015958138

Printed in the United States of America
Mankato, MN
June, 2016
PA02301

ABOUT THE AUTHOR
Sally McGraw is a freelance writer, newspaper columnist, blogger, and author. She lives in Minneapolis with her husband and two goofy cats.

ABOUT THE ILLUSTRATOR
Roger Stewart has been an artist and illustrator for more than 30 years. His first job involved drawing aircraft parts. Since then, he has worked in advertising, design, film, and publishing. Roger has lived in London, England, and Sydney, Australia, but he now lives on the southern coast of England.

Contents

CHAPTER ONE

Everyone Needs Water

Did you know that water keeps you alive? It not only tastes good when it is hot outside. Your body also needs water to stay healthy. Animals and plants also need water to live.

It might seem like there is enough water for everyone. But some places in the world deal with **drought**. Drought is when less rain falls than usual. Plants do not get enough water at these times. People sometimes run out of drinking water.

Drinking cold water helps keep us cool on hot days.

Oceans cover much of Earth. But people cannot drink ocean water. It has salt in it. Drinking too much salt makes people sick. We need to drink freshwater. Freshwater has no salt in it. Most lakes and rivers are freshwater. But Earth has a small amount of freshwater. And there are many people who need to drink it. The freshwater we have is very important.

Rain helps refresh our water supply.

Nature helps us reuse freshwater. It refreshes our supply through rain and snow. But humans sometimes use water too quickly. Earth cannot refresh it quickly enough. We sometimes run out of water. We should all do what we can to save our freshwater.

CHAPTER TWO

Good for Plants

Much of our water comes from rivers and streams. It is not salty. But sometimes it has other chemicals in it. These can make people sick. Chemicals are taken out before the water reaches our homes. The water that comes out of your tap has been cleaned.

Plants do not need tap water. Some of the chemicals that make people sick can help plants. You can use rainwater to water plants. You can save tap water from your tap for drinking.

A rain barrel makes it easy to gather rain. You can use it to water your family's

RAINWATER AND PLANTS

When water is cleaned, some chemicals are taken out. Others are put in to kill germs. Little pieces of dirt and leaves and some **acids** are taken out. Plants love water with acid. They do not like water full of germ-killing chemicals. So water that has not been cleaned is perfect for them.

Water from a tap has been processed so it is safe to drink.

garden or a community garden. A rain barrel can hold many gallons. When you use water from it, you save tap water.

When you build a rain barrel, you also help stop **pollution**. Lots of rain might seem good for Earth. But too much can cause problems. When it rains too much, water flows along the ground. It picks up chemicals and germs. The water then goes into rivers and streams. They become polluted. If you gather rainwater, less flows along the ground. Less pollution goes into the rivers and streams. You have helped keep them cleaner.

Rainwater that flows over the ground can become polluted.

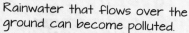

CHAPTER THREE

Good for People

Rain barrels help nature. They are also helpful to people. You can use rainwater to wash your dog, your windows, or your family's car. This water does not need to be cleaned. People pay for the tap water that comes into their homes. So using water from a rain barrel helps people save money.

If you live in a place that has drought, your town may have rules about using tap water. These rules help save the water everyone shares. Rules such as these usually say you cannot water your

You do not need to use tap water to wash a car.

lawn or wash your car with tap water. Having a rain barrel full of water means you can keep doing those things. Just make sure to check if your area has any rules about how you can use your rain barrel.

Maybe you live somewhere that gets a lot of rain. When lots of water sits near the spot where a house meets the ground, it can damage the house. A rain barrel keeps the rainwater that falls on your roof from hitting the ground. The water does not pool up next to your house.

A rain barrel lets you gather the rain that falls onto your roof.

Your rain barrel might make people curious. They may choose to build their own rain barrels. You can become a leader by showing other people how important it is to care for nature.

CHAPTER FOUR

Building a Rain Barrel

RAIN CHAIN

Some people do not have downspouts. This does not mean they cannot use rain barrels. They can use rain chains. Rain chains are long chains. They hang down from the edges of roofs. You can place one over where you plan to put your rain barrel. It will drip rainwater into your barrel.

Before you start making your rain barrel, you will need help from an adult. Your finished rain barrel will gather the water that flows off a roof. It will come down through gutters and a **downspout**. Talk to an adult about the best spot for your rain barrel.

Once you have a place to put your rain barrel, you need supplies. You might have some of the materials at your home. If not, a hardware store is a good place to buy them. Let's get started!

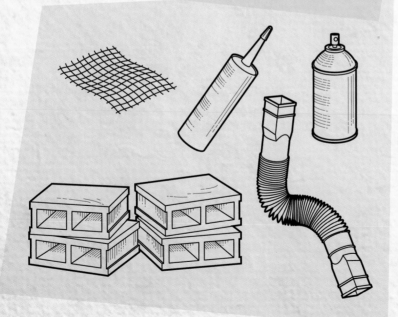

MATERIALS

- ☐ Large plastic garbage can with lid
- ☐ Ruler
- ☐ Handheld cordless drill
- ☐ **Spigot**
- ☐ 2 rubber **washers**
- ☐ 2 metal washers
- ☐ Nut that fits around the end of the spigot
- ☐ Tube of **sealant**
- ☐ Piece of mesh fabric big enough to cover the garbage can opening
- ☐ Paint that works on plastic (optional)
- ☐ 4 to 8 **cinder blocks**
- ☐ Downspout extension (optional)

INSTRUCTIONS

STEP 1: Have an adult cut an opening in the garbage can's lid. The hole should be as big as the end of the downspout.

STEP 2: Have an adult drill a hole 3 inches (8 cm) from the bottom of the can. The end of the spigot should fit in this hole.

STEP 3: Have an adult drill two small holes near the top of the can. These will let out any extra water.

STEP 4: You are now ready to put your rain barrel together. Put a metal washer onto the end of the spigot.

STEP 5: Put sealant on the flat side of the rubber washer. Then put the rubber washer onto the end of the spigot. The side with sealant should face away from the metal washer.

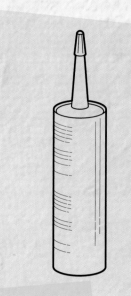

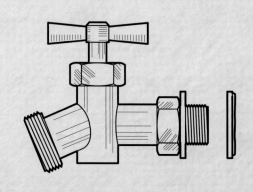

STEP 6: Put the spigot in the hole near the bottom of the garbage can. Press hard so the sealant sticks to the can. The sealant will keep water from leaking out of your rain barrel.

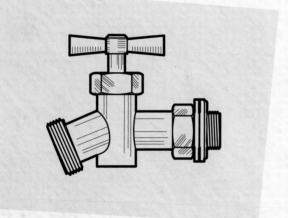

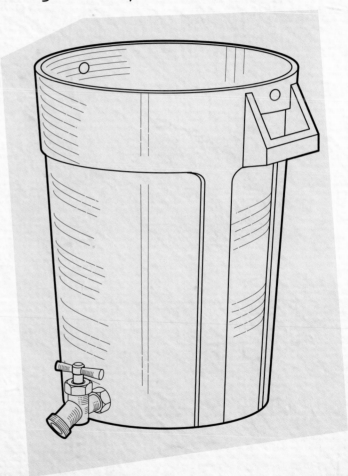

STEP 7: Inside the can, put the other rubber washer on the end of the spigot. Then put the other metal washer over that.

STEP 8: Put the nut on after the metal washer. Spin it until it is tight. This will keep the spout from popping out.

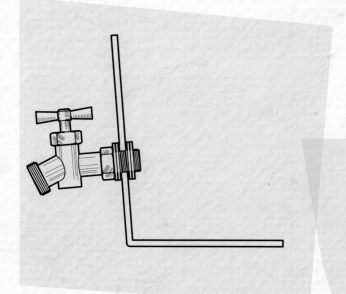

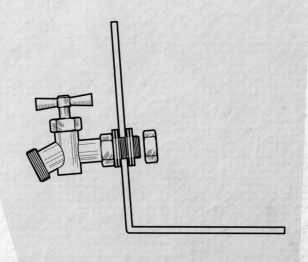

STEP 9: If you would like, paint the outside of your new rain barrel. Make sure to use paint that will stick to the plastic.

STEP 10: Put the mesh fabric on top of the can.

STEP 11: Put the lid on top of the fabric.

STAYING CLEAN

The mesh fabric helps keep your water clean. It keeps out leaves, sticks, and bugs. You can also add .5 cups (.2 L) of vegetable oil to the water. This helps keep bugs from laying eggs on top of the water.

STEP 12: Stack the cinder blocks into the shape of a rectangle. Make sure the blocks create a good base for your rain barrel. You do not want it to tip over. Make sure the spigot sits high enough that you can fit a watering can under it.

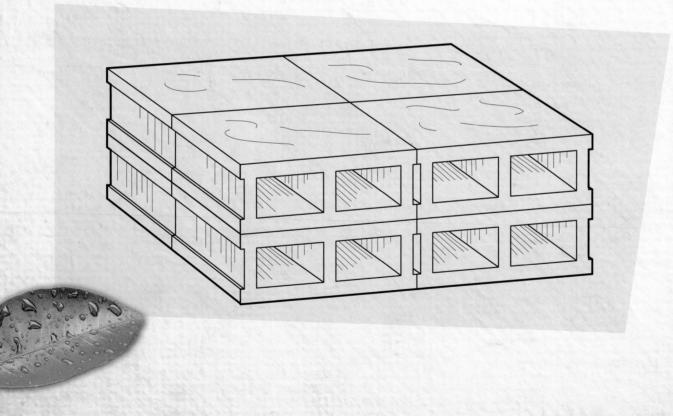

BREAKING BARREL

Make sure your rain barrel does not get too full. It may burst after a while. If your family members are worried about this, they can spend a little more on a heavy-duty barrel.

STEP 13: Have an adult adjust the downspout so that it feeds water into your rain barrel. You might need to use a downspout extension.

STEP 14: Check your rain barrel regularly. Clear away things such as branches from the top of the barrel. Make sure the screen is still intact. Also, check to make sure the barrel is not leaking. If it is, have an adult help you fix the issue. Empty the barrel out if the weather gets cold. The water inside could freeze and ruin the barrel. It is also good to clean the barrel out at least once per year. Doing so helps keep the water in the barrel clean.

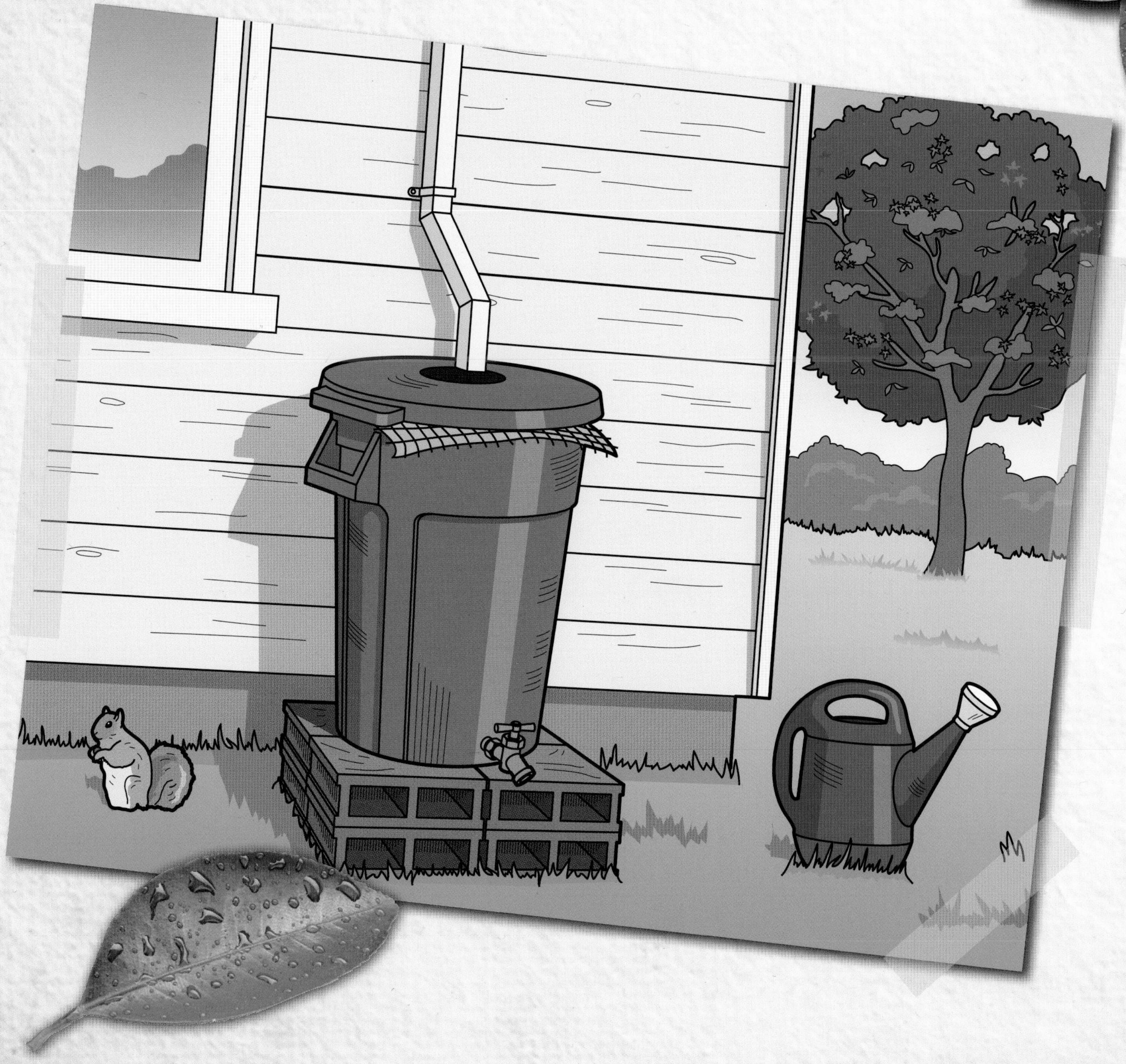

GLOSSARY

acids (AS-ids) Acids are sour substances. Acids are taken out when drinking water is purified.

cinder blocks (SIN-dur bloks) Cinder blocks are large bricks, usually with holes in their centers. People can use cinder blocks to raise their rain barrels off the ground.

downspout (DOWN-SPOWT) A downspout is a pipe that takes rainwater off the roof of a house and moves it toward the ground. A downspout might gush water during a thunderstorm.

drought (DROWT) A drought happens when it does not rain for a long, long time. A drought can make farmers' crops die.

pollution (puh-LOO-shuhn) Pollution happens when dangerous or unhealthy stuff gets into the water or the air. Throwing trash in a river is one form of pollution.

sealant (SEE-luhnt) Sealant is a thick liquid that becomes hard when it dries. Sealant helps keep water from leaking out of containers.

spigot (SPIG-uht) A spigot is a faucet. A rain barrel's spigot allows people to get water out of the barrel.

washers (WAW-shers) Washers are round, flat pieces with holes in their centers. Washers help keep things from leaking.

TO LEARN MORE

In the Library

Beatrice, Hollyer. *Our World of Water: Children and Water around the World*. New York: Henry Holt, 2009.

Brown, Renata Fossen. *Gardening Lab for Kids: 52 Fun Experiments to Learn, Grow, Harvest, Make, Play, and Enjoy Your Garden*. London: Quarry Books, 2014.

Geiger, Beth. *Clean Water*. San Diego, CA: Sally Ride Science, 2009.

On the Web

Visit our Web site for links about rain barrels:
childsworld.com/links

Note to Parents, Teachers, and Librarians:
We routinely verify our Web links to make sure
they are safe and active sites. So encourage
your readers to check them out!

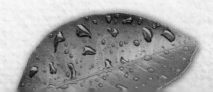

INDEX